early praise

AMERICA
according to
CONNOR
GIFFORD

NATHANIEL PHILBRICK
Pulitzer Finalist, Mayflower

"Connor Gifford writes my kind of history. This is a fun and inspirational book."

TIM RUSSERT
NBC, Meet the Press

"A distinctive American perspective from a unique young man."

JERRY STILLER & ANNE MEARA
acclaimed actors and authors

"A unique must read. Thank you Connor!"

VERN LAUX
National Public Radio Commentator

"History as it has never been written before. Lively and uplifting."

KEN JOHNSON
Publisher

"Insightful, interesting and inspiring."

MARCIA POOL RUTHERFORD
Educator/Mother of child with Autism

"Fantastic and intuitive."

To: Jack & Jane

AMERICA
according to
CONNOR GIFFORD

with
Victoria Harris

Connor Gifford

Hargrave Press LLC
Nantucket

For Grammie Anne
and Bop
CG

For Ned and Stephanie
Kate and Nathan
VH

Published by Hargrave Press LLC

For information about book clubs, interviews and personal appearances by the authors please visit connorgifford.com and hargravepress.com

First printing, May, 2008
Printed in the U.S.A.
ISBN: 978-0-9817195-0-4

Publisher's note: Connor's quotations of historical figures are faithful representations of what might actually have been said.

Profiles and drawings: Connor Gifford
Book Design and Co-Author: Victoria Harris
Artistic Director: Julie Gifford
Layout, photo page xi, Nathan Coe
Photo page 138, Maryann Anagnos

Hargrave Press LLC
P.O. Box 524 Nantucket MA 02554
585.260.4000 hargravepress.com

FOREWORD

PROLOGUE

IN THE BEGINNING

The First Americans 3
The Mayflower Arrives 5
Anne Hutchinson 9
The Original 13 11
First Great Awakening 13
Benjamin Franklin 15

ROAD TO FREEDOM

The Tipping Point 19
Writing the Declaration 21
Five-Pointed Star 25
Creating Our Symbol 27
Abigail and John 29
Thirst for Freedom 31
American Legend 33
The Bill of Rights 35

GROWING PAINS

Man of the People 39
To the Pacific! 41
Duel in the Park 43
"O! Say Can You See" 45
Second Great Awakening 47
Black Daniel Webster 49
Manifest Destiny 51
Lucretia Mott 53
Moses of Her People 55
Fugitive Slave Law 57

I Want To Be Free! 61
A Nation Divided 63
Glory Days 65
The Turning Point 67
Bobby Lee 69
Free at Last? 71
Jim Crow 73
New Hope 77
Third Great Awakening 79
A Beautiful Woman 81
Plessy vs. Ferguson 83

AMERICA TAKES THE LEAD

Turn of the Century 89
Over There 91
Thanks Woodrow! 93
Can You Spare a Dime? 95
So Long 97
Déjà vu 99
I Like Ike! 101
Mass Destruction 103
The World Unites 105
A Curtain Descends 107
A True Heroine 109
Free At Last! 113
The Cold War Continues 115
Four Dead in Ohio 117
National Nightmare 119
The Wall Falls! 121
9/11 123
Iraq 125

MY BIGGEST CONCERNS 127

HOPE FOR THE FUTURE 133

READER GROUPS 141

foreword

I first met Connor Gifford through my daughter Kate, and her husband Nathan, in January of 2007. One unforgettable day, Connor and I got to talking about how much he loves American history, and that is when this book was born.

I asked Connor, "Is your ability to identify with people who take risks—and scorned for being 'different'—inspired by your having Down Syndrome?" His answer was an unequivocal, "No."

Connor's love of our nation's history transcends any attempt to find a sentimental explanation.

Over the past ten months, we have spent countless hours discussing ideas, and doing research. As Connor worked on his profiles and drawings, I designed and edited the book, and provided the headings and the sidebars.

Thank you, dear Connor, for being in my life, and inspiring me to put the writing of my novel on hold so that I could devote myself to this life-changing experience!

Early on, we decided to keep the making of our book "in the family." Mom Julie, a gifted artist, helped Connor develop his original drawings, and was invaluable to us in every way imaginable, as was Dad Chuck with historic advice, and my son-in-law Nathan with the layout.

The making of this innovative vision of America was full of serendipity. Andrew arrived just when we needed his creative eye; Nick with his recording expertise; Kate at Plum TV with her interviews; and Debbie with Book Expo. Amy, Lou, Robert, Kathy, Nancy, the media and the book stores—so many in Nantucket have been supportive, especially Nathaniel, Jerry, Anne, Tim, and Vern.

You are all a special part of history in the making, a book that is a tonic for our times!

Victoria Harris
Nantucket
May, 2008

prologue

Hi! I'm Connor Gifford.
Welcome!

Right now I am living on the island of Nantucket. My parents are Julie and Chuck Gifford.

I have two brothers: Cameron who is 23 and Hunter who is 22. I am 26, the oldest, and I love my life!

During my growing up years, we lived in Perrysburg, Ohio where I graduated from high school in 2002.

Some subjects I did poorly in, like math and science. But, I succeeded in English and my favorite of all, history.

It all started in 8th grade in my mid-teens. In history class many kids were sleeping, doodling, and failing to make notes.

And that's the problem today. Kids are being taught with dates and timelines.

They do not go to the past and say, "Oh, I know why they did this!"

They can't picture themselves
back then.

But, I learned something from
history. As I read on, and learned
more, I felt that I was in their shoes.

I like learning about America and
people who really made a difference;
who said, "Hey, here I am!"

Ben Franklin, Harriet Tubman,
Thomas Jefferson, Rosa Parks,
and Dr. Martin Luther King, Jr.

It is important that all Americans
understand that what happened
in the past really matters.

We have to learn from
our mistakes.

I would like to thank my very good friend Victoria Harris for helping me find my voice.

Thank you Mom and Dad for supporting me in all that I do.

Thank you Kate, Nathan, and all the book stores.

And thank you God for giving me the gift of Down Syndrome.

Connor Gifford
Nantucket
May, 2008

in the
beginning

the first americans

1492

Before the white men arrived,
Indian tribes were everywhere.
They lived in teepees.

They hunted buffalo for clothing,
for food, to make their homes.
They used all of the animal and

wasted nothing.

Each tribe—from their hunting
to their ceremonies—
was unique.

Their spirit and their culture
guided them along the way. They
believed that the land was sacred,

and that no one owns it.

That made them
different from

us.

"Honor the sacred.
Honor the earth,
our Mother.
Honor the Elders.
Honor all with whom
we share the Earth:
four-leggeds, two-
leggeds, winged ones,
swimmers, crawlers,
plant and rock people.
Walk in balance
and beauty."

Unknown Native
American Elder

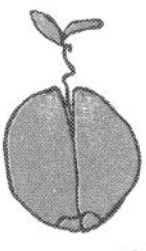

the mayflower arrives 1620

The Pilgrims came here from
England because they wanted
to practice freedom of religion,

and seek a better life.

Times were tough at first. Actually,
they almost went back to England.
But Squanto, an Indian, said,

"Do not be afraid of us.
We welcome you to this land.
We will help you grow crops."

And, of course, after the first
harvest the Pilgrims and Indians
celebrated the first Thanksgiving.

But there was trouble on the horizon.
A chief, called Philip, was upset that
the English wanted more land,

and more power.

So in 1675, he rebelled and the Indians
attacked settlers wherever they lived.
This was called King Philip's War.

"In two or three months' time, half of their company died...wanting houses and other comforts; being infected with the scurvy and other diseases...there died some times two or three a day."

- Pilgrim leader William Bradford

"My ancestors didn't come over on the Mayflower, but they were here to meet the boat."

- Will Rogers

THE INDIANS LOST

and they never recovered.

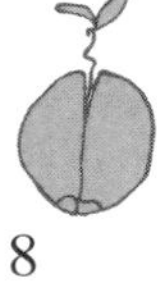

anne hutchinson 1637

Anne was born in England. She set
sail for the New World, in 1634, with
her husband, a minister, and their

15 children. Three died on the trip.

They lived in what is now Boston,
and Anne did bible studies and talks
in her home with women and men.

She believed that religion has to
do with more than the Bible.
It is how you live your life.

She opened minds to different ways
to practice religion, to women's
rights, and to the rights of Indians.

Women did *not* do that.

In her community, people complained,
"We don't like what Anne is doing!"
So, they put charges against her.

And she was banished.

"Mrs. Hutchinson,
the sentence of the
court you hear is that
you are banished from
out of our jurisdiction
as being a woman not
fit for our society, and
are to be imprisoned
til the court shall send
you away."

- Trial of Anne Hutchinson
Court of Newton, 1637

Anne and her family relocated to Rhode Island. When her husband died, she moved to Long Island.

One day, the local Indians attacked Anne and her children. The only survivor was her daughter Susannah.

Susannah lived because the Indians fell in love with her red hair. They changed her name to Autumn Leaf.

We must never forget
Ann Hutchinson.

SHE WAS
OUR FOUNDING
MOTHER

the original 13

1732

Starting in New England, there was Massachusetts and New Hampshire. Vermont and Maine came later.

The Duke of York had a friend by the name of Jersey, and they got together and created New York and New Jersey.

William Penn, who was a Quaker, was given land by the Indians, and he called it Pennsylvania.

Further down the Middle Colonies, there was Rhode Island, Connecticut, Maryland and Delaware.

Virginia, North and South Carolina, and Georgia had plantations. They grew tobacco, and they had slaves.

In the North, merchants prospered in cities like New York and Boston, and there were many farms.

At this time, they also had slaves and indentured servants—whites, black and Indians—who worked in their houses.

It took more than 100 years after the Pilgrims arrived for the first 13 Colonies to be created.

first great awakening 1730-1750

At this time, the colonists had scattered to many different places, and they did not go to church.

Then, the Great Awakening began.

The Revivalists said, "We need change in our churches." Many new kinds of worship started, like the Presbyterians.

Jonathan Edwards, a minister, started speaking, and people went crazy. His words were like a song that I love:

"God is an awesome God,
he reigns from heaven above,
with wisdom, power and love."

Everyone started going to church, and when they got together, they discussed things like slavery,

and being ruled by England.

During Jonathan Edwards' most famous speech, *Sinners in the hands of an Angry God,* the congregation was reported to cry, faint and go into convulsions.

benjamin franklin 1760

This was a time when scientists
started thinking about how
things work.

Ben Franklin was very smart.
He flew his kite in big storms,
and discovered electricity.

But, there is more to Franklin than
electricity. He was also an author,
printer, inventor, and diplomat.

When he was 20 years old, Franklin
created 13 Virtues. And he tried to
live by them all of his life.

He was part of the Enlightenment.

The Enlightenment said that
we should think for ourselves,
and ask questions like,

"Why are we so connected
to England? Why not be
independent?"

FRANKLIN'S
13 VIRTUES:

TEMPERANCE
SILENCE
ORDER
RESOLUTION
FRUGALITY
INDUSTRY
SINCERITY
JUSTICE
MODERATION
CLEANLINESS
TRANQUILITY
CHASTITY
HUMILITY

Ben Franklin, Thomas Jefferson, and John Adams designed the Great Seal of the United States. The motto says,

> "Rebellion to tyrants is obedience to God."

I believe that Benjamin Franklin is the most underrated figure in American history.

road to
freedom

the tipping point

1770 -1776

Basically, some were saying, "Let's be nice to England." But Ben Franklin and John Adams were saying, "Let's not."

Our patience was being taxed, day by day. First, the Boston Massacre. English troops killed five innocent citizens.

Then, King George appointed somebody Governor. He passed a tax on sugar, and no sugar traded. Then, mailing stopped.

Without the King knowing it, the Sons of Liberty dressed up like Indians, and they dumped all the tea into Boston Harbor.

King George was outraged, and sent the Redcoats—as the English soldiers were called—to Lexington and Concord.

A young man named Paul Revere yelled, "The British are coming! The British are coming!"

And the Revolutionary War began.

"Listen my children
and you shall hear
Of the midnight ride
of Paul Revere,
On the eighteenth of
April, in Seventy-five;
Hardly a man is now
alive who remembers
that famous day and
year."

- *Paul Revere's Ride*
Henry Wadsworth
Longfellow

writing the declaration 1776

Now, this gets even better!
In the movie *1776*, the question
at the Continental Congress was,

"Who is going to write the
Declaration of Independence?"

Robert Sherman said, "I cannot do
this." He was confused as to what
was a quill, and what was a pen.

Robert Livingston said, "I cannot
write it." He was from New York,
and his handwriting was so sloppy.

And then, Benjamin Franklin said,
"I cannot do it either."

Only one was left, Thomas Jefferson.
John Adams pursued Jefferson, but
he said "No, I want to see my wife!"

And a heated argument broke out.

"We hold these truths to be self-evident: that all men are created equal; that they are endowed by their creator with inherent and [certain] inalienable rights; that among these are life, liberty, and the pursuit of happiness."

- Thomas Jefferson

Congress did not end the Slave Trade in America until 1808

One day, Jefferson was playing his violin—he was a musician—and Franklin and Adams came to see him.

Also, at this point in time—it seems a bit weird at first—but Franklin fell asleep on Jefferson's bed!

But guess what? John Adams had something up his sleeve.

His wife Abigail was best friends with Martha Jefferson and she said, "Come to Philadelphia to see your husband."

Thomas Jefferson was so inspired by his wife, that he finally sat down and wrote the Declaration of Independence!

It says that "All men are created equal," but, after much discussion, they finally decided that this did not include...

SLAVES

and

WOMEN

five-pointed star

1776

Betsy Ross lived in Philadelphia and was a seamstress. One day, George Washington came to visit her Uncle.

Betsy showed him how to make a five-pointed star. And that really impressed Washington.

So, he asked her to design a flag for America. Many people think this is a myth, but I personally like the story.

The Stars and Stripes symbolize freedom and justice for all. This is why I believe that

nobody should ever burn our flag.

"My stars and my stripes...are bright with cheer, brilliant with courage, firm with faith, because you have made them so out of your heart."

- Franklin Knight Lane

creating our symbol 1776-1782

At the Second Continental Congress, an argument began about what the national symbol should be.

Benjamin Franklin wanted a turkey. Robert Sherman thought maybe a snake. John Adams wanted an eagle.

Franklin said the turkey was brave, but John Adams said that the bald eagle was majestic, intelligent and bold.

They argued for six years! Finally everybody stopped arguing, and that is how we chose the eagle.

John Adams won.

Again.

The Bald Eagle is the symbol on the Great Seal, the president's flag and the one dollar bill.

abigail and john

1777

What Abigail Adams did really
set her husband John Adams apart.
She gave him encouragement.

While he was talking about his ideas
at the Second Continental Congress,
they wrote to each other a lot.

"How are the kids? Are they OK?"
he asked. He told her that he needed
salt peter so soldiers' rifles would fire.

Abigail, in return, told John that
she needed pins because she and
her lady friends were quilting.

When John got her the pins, she
kept her word, and made sure
that he got his salt peter.

What she so wanted was that one
day John would be successful.
And to this I say,

"Way to go Abigail!"

"If particular care and
attention is not paid
to the ladies, we are
determined to foment
a rebellion, and will not
hold ourselves bound
by any laws in which
we have no voice or
representation."

- Abigail Adams

Abigail got her wish
for her husband.
John Adams was our
first Vice President
and second President.

thirst for freedom 1778

During the Revolutionary War, a young woman was with her husband right in the middle of a big battle.

She was a servant, and her job was to bring pitchers of water to the tired and thirsty soldiers.

When her husband was shot, she stood her ground, and took over firing his cannon. How brave that was!

When George Washington learned what she had done, he made her a sergeant in his Army.

From that time on, everyone called her Molly Pitcher, and she became a legend.

"These are times that try men's souls."

- Molly Pitcher

american legend 1789

Washington was tall. He had white
hair. He had curls going up his ears,
and a pony tail in the back.

The most famous story that I can
recall, is the one about the day he
chopped down a cherry tree.

"I cannot tell a lie," he said.
Now we may think this is a myth,
but this is the way he lived.

He was a great general. He led us
in the Revolutionary War. Then,
he became our first president.

And do you know why he
never ran for a third term?

He did not want to be a ruler.

"I walk on untrodden ground. There is scarcely any part of my conduct which may not hereafter be drawn into precedent."

"I have no other view than to promote the public good, and am unambitious of honors not founded in the approbation of my Country."

- George Washington

"My mother was the most beautiful woman I ever saw. All I am I owe to my mother."

"My first wish is to see this plague of mankind, war, banished from the earth."

"Over grown military establishments are to be regarded as particularly hostile to republican liberty."

"Some day, following the example of the United States of America, there will be a United States of Europe."

"I can only say that there is not a man living who wishes more sincerely than I do to see a plan adopted for the abolition of slavery."

- George Washington

the bill of rights

1791

After the Constitution was written, they realized it did not go far enough. So they created the Bill of Rights.

These are actually the first Ten Amendments to the Constitution.

The First Amendment insures freedoms such as speech, religion, press and the right to bear arms.

But, what the Bill of Rights did *not* say was, "If you get a gun, do not turn around and kill somebody."

They left that

out.

"We have the Bill of Rights. What we need is a Bill of Responsibilities."

- Bill Maher

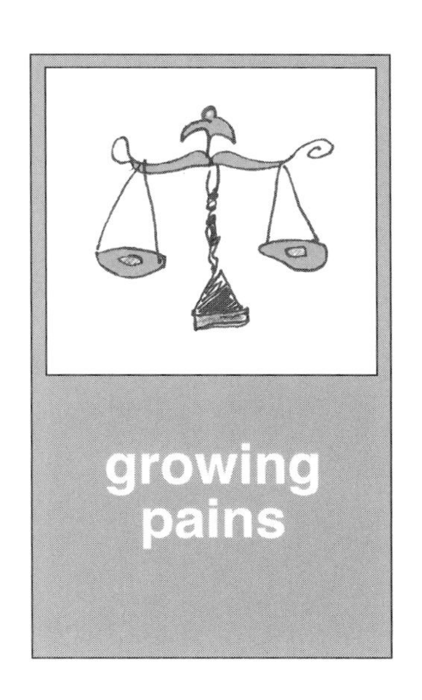
growing
pains

man of the people

1803

He was actually a very nice guy—
though a bit shy at times—
and he played his violin a lot.

He designed his house in Virginia,
and farmed his land with slaves.
But, he did not like slavery.

People loved Thomas Jefferson
because he wrote the Declaration
of Independence.

He had been secretary of state
and vice president, and now it was
his time to lead the country.

When Jefferson became
president, his best idea was
the expansion of America.

"I think this is the most extraordinary collection of talent, of human knowledge, that has ever been gathered together at the White House, with the possible exception of when Thomas Jefferson dined alone."

- President Kennedy's toast at dinner for Nobel Laureates, 1962

to the pacific!

1804-1806

At this point in time, America was only 17 States that ended at the Appalachian Mountains.

President Jefferson wanted to expand westward, and find out what was out there.

So he asked Meriwether Lewis and William Clark to lead an expedition into the unknown.

They brought back their diaries, and stories about Indians they met along the way.

Sacagawea, for instance. She was only 17 when she went to the Pacific with Lewis and Clark.

She was guide and translator. They tasted the food, made many maps, and drew pictures of plants.

The expedition was a big success. People were like, "Wow, this is great, new land. Let's try it out!"

When Jefferson became President, most Americans lived within 50 miles of the Atlantic Ocean.

Congress appropriated $2,500 to fund the Lewis and Clark expedition.

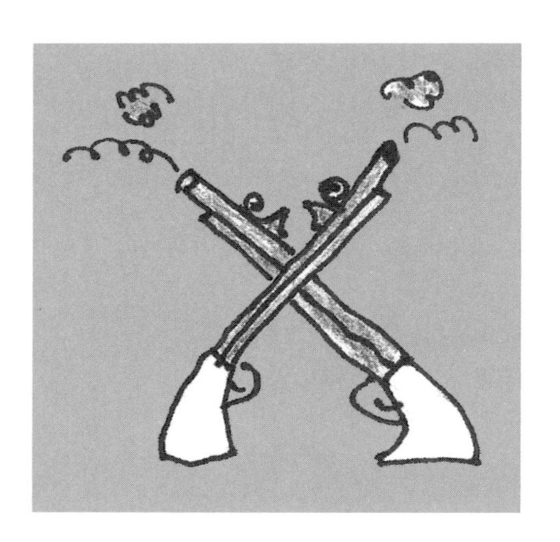

duel in the park

1804

When Washington was president,
a big rivalry was going on between
two of our Founding Fathers.

Alexander Hamilton was smart and
self-made. He was our first secretary
of the treasury when he was just 32.

Aaron Burr was tall, he had red hair,
and was born from a wealthy family.
Hamilton was very jealous of him.

Burr was running against Jefferson
for president. Hamilton did not like
Jefferson, but he hated Burr.

So, he helped to elect Jefferson!
When Burr became vice president,
he and Hamilton kept arguing.

They didn't stop until Burr pulled
out his gun, and next thing you know,
Alexander Hamilton was dead!

Burr went out west, and was charged
with treason. He then spent the rest
of his life alone. A frail, old man.

Alexander Hamilton said of Aaron Burr:

"He is bold, enterprising, and intriguing, and I feel it is a religious duty to oppose his career."

"o! say can you see" 1814

Baltimore Harbor.
Smoke everywhere.
Bombs bursting in the air.

A young poet by the name
of Francis Scott Key saw this,
with his own eyes, during

the War of 1812. America was
at war with England again!

The words that he wrote down
were made into a song, and it
became our National Anthem.

"The Star Spangled Banner"
says that we cannot be defeated
because we are

"the land of the free
and the home of the brave."

The music for The *Star Spangled Banner* is a popular British drinking song by John Stafford Smith.

It became our National Anthem in 1931.

second great awakening 1800-1830

At this point in time, we needed to think about the bigger picture. And what we had become.

There was a big, new interest in religion, and preachers excited large crowds at revival meetings.

Some were at camps where people danced, and sang, and got carried away with the speeches.

New churches started everywhere.

There was much talk about slavery, rights for women, prisons, alcohol, and how we were going to grow.

The people thought that it was God's will that America should expand out west.

So, we did.

New Christian movements that began at this time include:

Disciples of Christ, Seventh-Day Adventists and Latter Day Saints (also known as the Mormons).

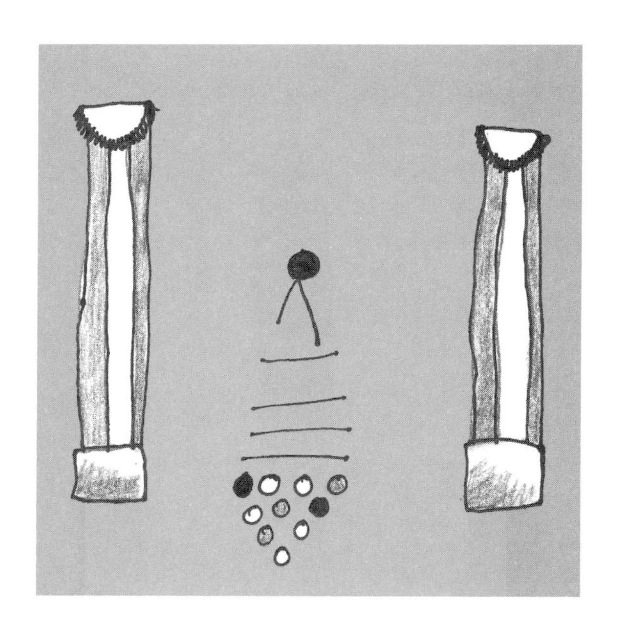

black daniel webster 1841

His mother was a slave. His father was a white man. And they had a son named Frederick.

He tried three different times to escape, but failed. Finally, he succeeded and went to Philadelphia, then New York.

When he was 23, he came to Nantucket, and in the Great Hall of the Atheneum, Frederick Douglass spoke about

why slavery is wrong.

He was really nervous, but it was this speech that made him famous. He was a great public speaker, and an author.

Douglass helped Lucretia Mott with the first Women's Rights Convention, and he signed the Declaration of Sentiments.

He also published a newspaper called *The North Star*—the star that the slaves followed at night as they escaped.

"At the end of his speech in Nantucket, it was clear that a powerful new voice had been raised, one that demonstrated how high a former slave could stretch in a demonstration of his humanity."

- Douglass biographer William McFeely

manifest destiny

1840s

During the Second Great Awakening,
people felt that we were destined
to expand from ocean to ocean.

This led President Andrew Jackson
to promote the annexation of
Texas from Mexico.

There were two leaders at this time:
Santa Anna and Steven F. Austin.
These two men were bitter enemies.

Mexico owned Texas
but America wanted it.
So, we went to war.

The big battle was the Alamo. Daniel
Boone, Davy Crockett, and Austin
were all there. It was pure bloodshed.

A soldier yelled,
"Remember the Alamo!"
And we have. Ever since.

The U.S. won the Mexican War.
And that is how we got Texas
and California.

"It is perfectly heathenish, a filibustering toward heaven by the great western route. No; they may go their way to their manifest destiny, which I trust is not mine."

- Henry David Thoreau

lucretia mott

1848

She was born on the island of
Nantucket, and became the first
female Quaker minister.

In this time, before the Civil War,
women were struggling, and they
needed to be heard big time.

She got together with Elizabeth
Cady Stanton, and they created the
first Women's Rights Convention.

I love this woman Lucretia Mott!
She wrote down her thoughts about
her right to vote, and to do business.

That was very brave because, at
that time, women were not equal.

Her whole name was
Lucretia Coffin Mott.

My grandmother's side in
Nantucket—the Greenleafs—
are related to the Coffins.

So, Lucretia Mott is my ancestor!

At the first Women's Rights Convention at Seneca Falls, New York, 100 women and men—including Frederick Douglass—signed the Declaration of Sentiments. Its opening line was:

"We hold these truths to be self-evident; that all men and women are created equal."

- Elizabeth Cady Stanton, 1848

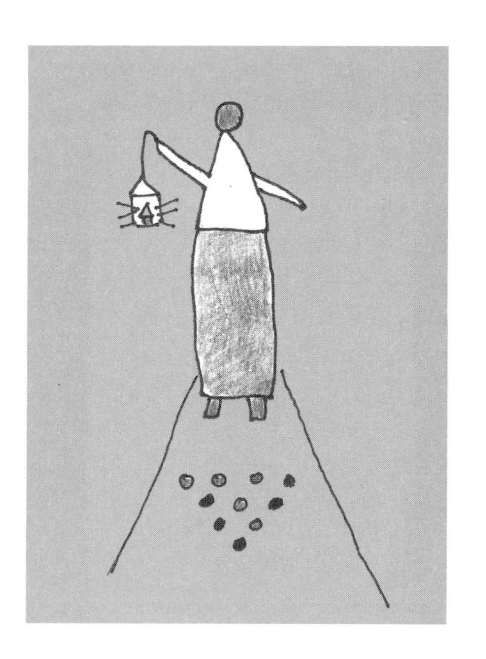

moses of her people

1849

Harriet Tubman was a slave.
She lived on a plantation, and
her childhood was not happy.

She had to watch over the baby
of one of her owners, and anytime
the baby cried, she got whipped.

She had many scars on her back.

When she was a teen, she saw her
owner abusing another slave, and
when she said something, he ran.

The owner threw a heavy weight,
and it hit Harriet. Her head was
swimming with blood.

That was not right!

After Harriet escaped, she was
the most famous conductor of
the Underground Railroad.

She risked her life, time and again,
to save her family, and to help other
slaves escape to Canada.

"I had crossed the line. I was free, but there was no one to welcome me to the land of freedom. I was a stranger in a strange land."

- Harriet Tubman

This is why she was called,
"The Moses of her people."

Harriet was a nurse. And would you believe it, she was even a Union spy during the Civil War!

There was a black man by the name of John Brown, and Harriet helped him with his raid on Harper's Ferry.

Then, she fought for women's rights.

When she was 93, and her body was frail, and she could not sleep at night because of her head injury,

Harriet Tubman passed away.

We must *never* ever forget Harriet. She was never afraid to risk her life, and to help other people to be

f r e e.

fugitive slave law

1850

The South was angry that slaves were escaping. So, they complained, and Congress came up with a law.

It said that if you saw an escaped slave, you had to send the slave back to the owner.

Anyone caught helping a runaway slave got six months in prison, and a $1,000 fine!

Brave people then actually went behind the back of Congress, and kept bringing slaves to freedom.

After the Fugitive Slave Law was passed, Harriet Beecher Stowe wrote the book, *Uncle Tom's Cabin.*

It was a huge success. It made people see that what happened in the book, actually happened in reality.

In fact, President Lincoln said, "So, you're the little woman who wrote the book that started this great war!"

After the Fugitive Slave Law was created, Canada became the final destination of most of the runaway slaves.

ELIZA'S ESCAPE TO FREEDOM:

Right on behind they [hounds and a posse of slavers] came; and, nerved with strength such as God gives only to the desperate, with one wild cry and flying leap, she vaulted sheer over the turbid current by the shore, on to the raft of ice beyond...The huge green fragment of ice on which she alighted pitched and creaked as her weight come on it, but she staid there not a moment. With wild cries and desperate energy she leaped to another and still another cake;— stumbling — leaping — slipping — springing upwards again! Her shoes are gone — her stockings cut from her feet — while blood marked every step; but she saw nothing, felt nothing, till dimly, as in a dream, she saw the Ohio side, and a man helping her up the bank.

- Harriet Beecher Stowe
  Uncle Tom's Cabin, 1852

i want to be free!

1857

Dred Scott was born a slave. He lived on a plantation in Virginia until he was bought by a doctor in Missouri.

The doctor took him North with him while he did his work in the Army. Then, they returned to Missouri.

And that is when Dred Scott said, "I want to be free."

He tried for ten years in one court after another in Missouri. Finally, he went all the way to the Supreme Court.

They decided that since blacks were not citizens, Dred Scott had no rights!

The judges were all white men.

Their decision was a real set-back for Abolition. The South used Dred Scott to keep slavery alive.

A few months after the decision, Dred Scott was finally freed. He died a year later in St. Louis.

In the ruling against Dred Scott, Supreme Court Chief Justice Taney wrote:

"All blacks had no rights which the white man were bound to respect; and that the negro might justly and lawfully be reduced to slavery for his benefit. He was bought and sold and treated as an ordinary article of merchandise and traffic, whenever profit could be made by it."

a nation divided

1860

The issue of slavery was so intense,
at this time, that it was the number
one topic of the presidential election.

Abraham Lincoln, the Republican,
was very tall and thin. He had a full-
grown beard, and wore a tall, black hat.

His biggest rival, Steven Douglas,
was really short, and he was, like,
full of himself. He said to the people,

"Who do you want to be your
president? Someone who
came from a log cabin?"

Lincoln was firm, he spoke slowly,
and he said, "Don't forget what is
going on here. It is not about me.

It is about slavery.
Our Union cannot survive
half-free, and half-slave."

After Lincoln was elected, seven
states in the South left the Union.
And the Civil War began.

Candidates in the
Election of 1860:

John C. Breckinridge
Southern Democrat

John Bell
Constitutional Union

Stephen A. Douglas
Northern Democrat

Abraham Lincoln
Republican

First States to secede:

South Carolina
Mississippi
Florida
Alabama
Georgia
Lousiana
Texas

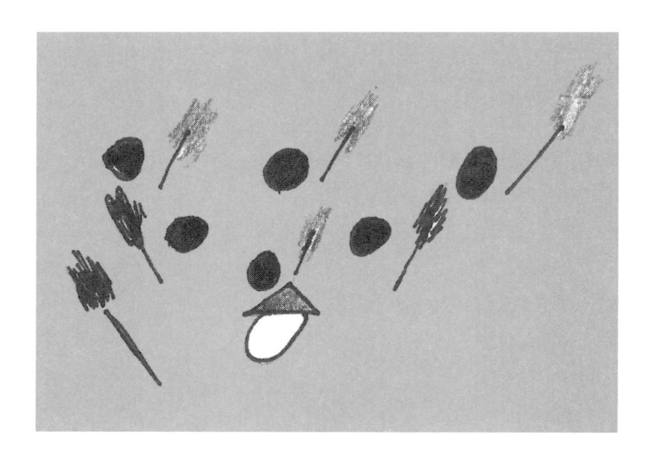

glory days

1863

The 54th Massachusetts Regiment
was led by Robert Gould Shaw.
He was young, and very handsome.

Shaw, at first, did not want to lead an all-black regiment, but his father convinced him to do it.

Shaw and his 600 men trained long and hard, and refused to be paid.

They were ordered to burn a small town in Georgia. Shaw said, "No!" and his boss threatened a court martial.

The town was shocked to see black soldiers. And they were screaming, "Stop! You cannot do this!"

The 54th then attacked a fort in South Carolina. Shaw was shot in his heart and his men fell one by one.

To this day, they remain
buried together in one grave.

This inspired the movie *Glory*.

"Confederate soldiers stripped Shaw's body and threw it into a common grave with his 116 fallen soldiers, believing this burial disgraced the young colonel. But his parents said they could hope for 'no holier place for Shaw than to be surrounded by his brave and dedicated soldiers.'"

- Military.com

the turning point

1863

In July, the Union soldiers went to
a place called Gettysburg to fight a
famous commander, Robert E. Lee.

The two sides fought furiously,
and on the third and final day of
the battle, Lee's troops retreated.

Lincoln wanted to honor the Union
dead at Gettysburg. So, in November,
he came to dedicate a new cemetery.

This is when he gave his famous
Gettysburg Address. "Four score
and seven years ago..."

His talk was short, and to the point.
He reminded everyone that our
Declaration of Independence says,

"All men are created equal."

After this, people who supported the
Confederates started to change sides.
They were tired of so many dying.

Their soldiers had only
peanuts to eat.

At the dedication of the cemetery at Gettysburg, the speech of the main speaker, Edward Everett, lasted two hours.

Lincoln's Gettysburg Address lasted about two minutes.

It consisted of 272 words.

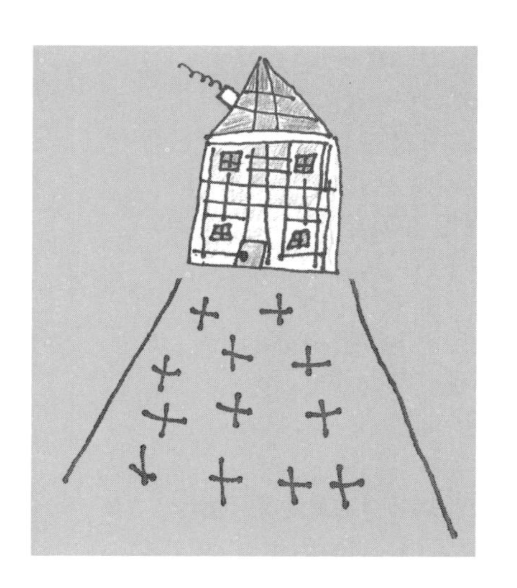

bobby lee

1865

He was short. He had gray hair,
and a full beard on his face.
And he was a famous general.

He was born in Virginia, and was
the type of guy who knew what he
wanted, and wasn't afraid to do it.

He did not want the South to secede,
but when Lincoln asked him to lead
the Union Army, he said, "No."

He then led the Confederate Army!
He won many victories, but what
happened in the end was a blow-out.

He wife, Mary Anna Curtis Lee, had
a big connection. She was Martha
Washington's great granddaughter.

They lived in her house, a big mansion,
in Arlington, Virginia. And when the
war ended, guess what happened?

Union soldiers changed Robert E.
Lee's front lawn into a burial ground.
This is Arlington National Cemetery.

The 300,000 plus members of our military and veterans buried at Arlington National Cemetery represent all of our wars through Iraq.

It is the site of the Tomb of the Unknowns and the grave of President John F. Kennedy.

Bobby Lee was a nickname for Robert E. Lee used by his soldiers.

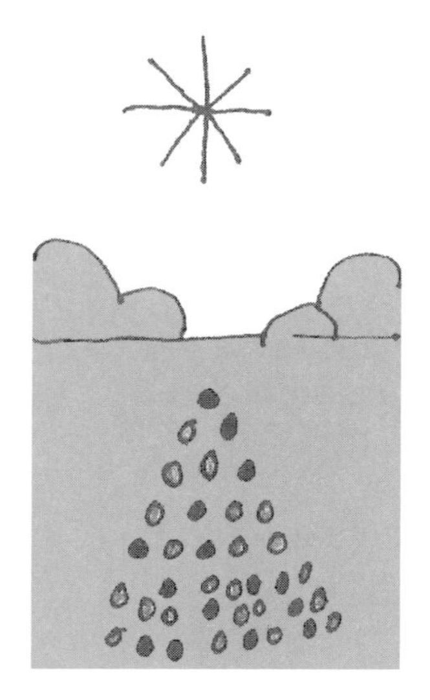

free at last? 1865

During the Civil War, Lincoln's Emancipation Proclamation freed slaves only in Confederate States.

When the war ended, the President wanted to make sure that slavery ended *everywhere* in America.

So, the 13th Amendment to the Constitution was created.

Four million slaves were now free. But no one knew, yet, about

seg re ga tion.

"Neither slavery nor involuntary servitude, except as a punishment for a crime whereof the party shall have been duly convicted, shall exist within the United States, or any place subject to their jurisdiction."

- The 13th Amendment

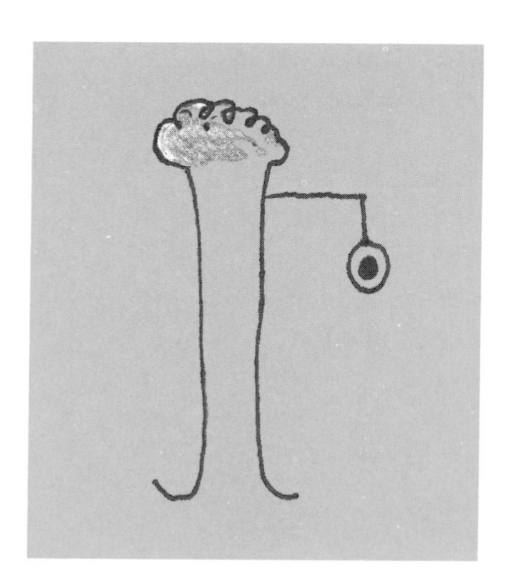

jim crow

1876

We don't really know where the
name Jim Crow came from, but
it meant that you were black.

Jim Crow Laws were a reaction
to Reconstruction, in the South,
after the Civil War ended.

Whites in the South kept coming
up with new ways to stop blacks
from being equal.

The Ku Klux Klan scared blacks
from voting. Blacks could not be
with whites on trains and buses.

If you were black, you could not
go to white schools, eat in white
restaurants, use white rest rooms,

or marry a white person.

Everything was affected.

Jim Crow Laws did not finally end in Southern and border states until 1965.

IT WAS CALLED SEPARATE, BUT EQUAL.

BUT IT WAS not equal.

new hope

1880-1920

Other than the Native Americans,
all of our ancestors originally
came from somewhere else.

In the beginning,
almost all of the people
came from England.

Then, after the Revolutionary War,
Germans showed up, along with the
Irish, Scots and Scandinavians.

When we went west in the 1800's,
the railroads needed workers, and they
brought Chinese and Japanese here.

The third wave started in the 1890s.
Millions of immigrants came from
Europe: the Italians, Poles and Jews.

Americans had mixed emotions
about all of these new people, and
there was a lot of prejudice.

But, when these immigrants arrived,
and they saw the Statue of Liberty,
it gave them new hope.

"Give me your tired, your poor, your huddled masses yearning to breathe free, The wretched refuse of your teeming shore. Send these, the homeless, tempest tost to me, I lift my lamp beside the golden door!"

- Inscription on the Statue of Liberty by Emma Lazarus, 1883

third great awakening 1880-1900

A big issue, at this point in time,
with there being so many new
immigrants, was urbanization.

It was a difficult journey from their
homelands to the new world. And when
they arrived, their lives totally changed.

They had to look for a place to live.
They had to find jobs, as well.
And that was not easy.

They had many problems such as
housing, transportation, food,
sanitation and crime.

If there was a fire, many people died.
20 or 30 people were packed in one
room, and they did not come out alive.

This was a time of many reformers.
They wanted to help these new people,
and religion played a big part in this.

This is when the YMCA was created,
as well as the Salvation Army, and
the Progressive Movement.

During this time, new
religious movements
began such as:

Christian Science
Jehovah's Witnesses
and Reformed Judaism

a beautiful woman

1893

She was a poet, a professor, and
she led the English Department
at Wellesley College.

One summer she went out West,
and during her visit she climbed
Pikes Peak with other teachers.

When she saw the view stretched
out far beyond her wildest dreams,
she was inspired to write a poem,

"America the Beautiful."

It expresses America so well that
it was an instant hit. In fact, many
wish it was our National Anthem.

Katharine Lee Bates was very self-
guided, and for 25 years she lived
with another woman.

Julia Ward Howe wrote the *Battle Hymn of the Republic* in 1862. She was a poet, abolitionist, and reformer.

In 1892, Francis Bellamy wrote *The Pledge of Allegiance.* He was a Christian Socialist and defrocked minister.

plessy vs. ferguson

1896

A young black man named Homer Plessy was on a train, and he would not give up his seat in the white section.

He was arrested, and when he went to court he said, "What did I do wrong? I just wanted to get home."

The case went to the Supreme Court. In Plessy vs. Ferguson, the court ruled against Homer. How could this be?

This terrible ruling upheld Jim Crow Laws. It made Separate but Equal, the Law of the Land!

After the Supreme Court ruled that Jim Crow Laws were O.K., Southerners got bolder.

There were white only and black only restaurants, health centers, rest rooms, schools, and so forth.

Nobody spoke up and said, "Stop this!" So, Separate but Equal went on, and on.

Justice John Harlan, the lone dissenter in the Supreme Court decision against Plessy wrote:

"Our Constitution is color-blind, and neither knows nor tolerates classes among citizens."

His fellow judges disagreed, and made Separate but Equal, the Law of the Land.

Jim Crow Laws finally ended due to: Brown vs. Board of Education in 1954; sit-ins at lunch counters; boycotts and Freedom Riders in the early 1960's; the Civil Rights Act in 1964; and the Voting Rights Act in 1965.

THE BLACKS WERE FREE

but, free to do what?

america takes the lead

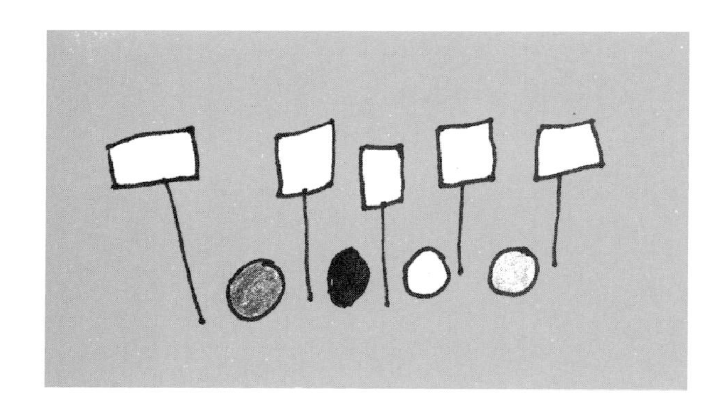

turn of the century

1900

At this point in time, we were getting
a sense of who we were, and we had
the first big business boom.

Carnegie started a monopoly with his
steel company...Rockefeller with oil.
There were many new inventions.

But, there were Jim Crow Laws
in the South. And immigrants had
problems with jobs and housing.

Workers started to unite, and
we had our first labor unions,
and our first strike.

The unions said, "We need better
working conditions. We need more
money. Our children need help."

The owners of the factories would
push them, and push them, until their
feet and hands would no longer work.

I am sick about it. I get so emotional
that I cry. Nobody should *ever* treat
a child unfairly, for any reason at all!

Investigative
journalists, called
"Muckrakers,"
brought attention
to issues such as:

Poverty,
Child labor,
Insane asylums,
Corruption,
Sweatshops,
Food safety,
Medical fraud,
Slums.

over there

1917

Europe was arguing over the assassination of an Archduke, and it led to World War I.

President Wilson wanted us to be neutral. So, those who wanted us to be in the war had to find an excuse.

They got it when a German U-boat sank the H.M.S. Lusitania, an ocean liner with many Americans on it.

But, Wilson did not go to war until he got a telegram that said Mexico was going to join Germany against us!

World War I was horrible. Soldiers had to deal with machine guns, barbed wire, tanks, and poison gas.

Soldiers breathed the gas, and it was a horrid, painful death. When our men came home, they had shell shock.

Wilson never wanted another war. He wanted America to join the League of Nations, but Congress refused.

During World War I military and civilian casualties totaled:
20 million dead and
21 million wounded.
America lost 116,708.

"In Flanders fields the poppies blow,
Between the crosses, row on row,
That mark our place; and in the sky
The larks still bravely singing, fly.
Scarce heard amid the guns below."

- Lt. Colonel John McCrae, M.D.

thanks woodrow! 1920

As I have been telling you,
it took a very long time for
women to gain the right to vote.

Finally, the 19th Amendment passed,
thanks to President Woodrow Wilson.
He pressured Congress to do it.

We must also thank: Elizabeth Cady
Stanton, Susan B. Anthony, Harriet
Tubman, Abigail Adams,

and, of course, Lucretia Mott!

Women's votes could now be counted.
They stepped out and became
a part of the bigger picture.

They were not as tied to home, thanks
to inventions like electricity, stoves,
refrigerators, and washing machines.

This transformed their lives.

The 19th Amendment said that: "The right of citizens of the United States to vote shall not be denied or abridged by the United States or by any State on account of sex."

It was ratified on August 18, 1920 when Tennessee voted yes.

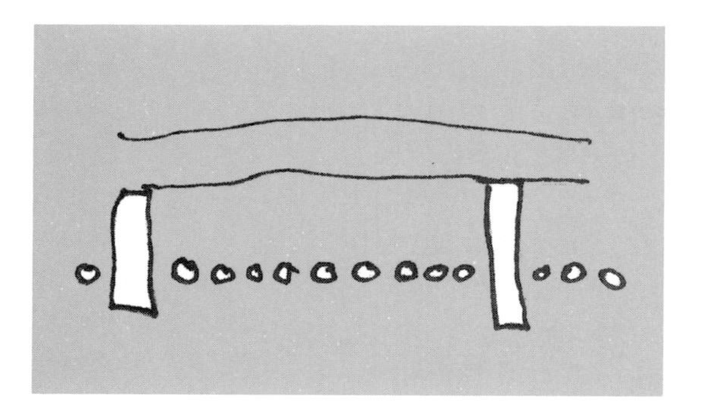

can you spare a dime? 1929

On a day called "Black Tuesday,"
the stock market crashed, and this
led to the Great Depression.

At this point in time, there was much
hardship, and much suffering. Many
lost their farms and businesses.

People, everywhere, were looking for
jobs, and there weren't any.

They would say, "Do you want this
bowl for a dime?" They were selling
what they had just to try and eat.

We needed hope to survive, and
we got the hope through President
Franklin Roosevelt's New Deal.

He helped us to regain what was lost.
He helped farmers, and he helped
people with housing and work.

But, he did not do anything
to end segregation.

Programs passed during the New Deal include:

Social Security,
FDIC - Federal Deposit Insurance Corporation,
FHA - Federal Housing Authority,
SEC - Securities and Exchange Commission

Brother, Can You Spare A Dime, by Woody Guthrie, was one of the most famous songs during the Great Depression.

so long

1941

A peaceful harbor in Hawaii.
Everybody going about their business,
until they heard airplanes and bombs.

Total shock! We were being attacked
by Japan at Pearl Harbor!

In Germany, one of the worst tyrants
ever, Adolph Hitler, rose to power,
and he wanted to rule the world.

We tried so much to be neutral,
but we had to enter World War II.

Hitler was a racist. He wanted to
get rid of the Jews, and gay men,
gypsies, even disabled people!

He created concentration camps.
All the people he didn't like were
sent to these camps.

They were whipped and starved.
And one by one they died horrible
deaths in gas chambers.

Total Deaths in
World War II
Military: 25 million
Civilian: 41 million
Holocaust: 6 million
U.S. Military: 446,000

"So long it's been
good to know you.
There's a mighty
big war that's got
to be won and we'll
get back together
again."

- Woody Guthrie, 1944

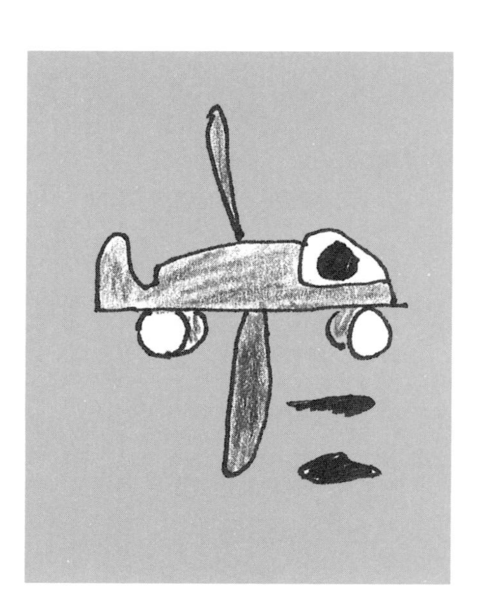

déjà vu

1942

A group of black pilots were at a base in Alabama, and these black pilots were training for the war.

But, they were segregated from the white pilots. So the 332nd Fighter Group was created.

They were called "Red Tails" because they painted the tails of their planes bright red.

It was like Shaw's Regiment in the Civil War, all over again. These men risked their lives, and they said,

"We are opening doors, and we are walking through them. We are not afraid to die for our country."

The Tuskegee airmen are
true,
American
heroes.

Six decades after World War II ended, The Tuskegee airmen were awarded the Congressional Gold Medal.

"The Tuskegee airmen left a segregated country to fight in war, and unfortunately returned to one that was still segregated. Though Hitler was defeated, prejudice was not... Today we are trying to right that wrong."

- House Speaker
Nancy Pelosi.

i like ike!

1944

He was born in Abilene, Kansas, one of six brothers. His mother Ida was religious, and did not believe in war.

But her son Dwight D. Eisenhower went to West Point, and he became Supreme Commander in WW II.

The Nazis were being tricked about where the invasion of France would occur. And once it started,

there was no turning back.

One of the things you never want to hear when going into battle are the words, “Bad weather.”

On June 5th, the weather at Normandy was terrible, and Eisenhower had to stop history’s biggest sea invasion.

The next day, when the weather cleared, he gave the order to attack and D-Day began.

The invasion of Normandy was the largest seaborne invasion in world history involving:
160,000 soldiers,
10,000 airplanes,
4,000 warships

“In the councils of government we must guard against the acquisition of unwarranted influence...by the military-industrial complex.”

- Farewell Address by President Eisenhower, January, 1961

After the war, Ike—as he was called—
became President. When he retired he
made his home in Gettysburg and

he joined the Presbyterian Church.

We have to thank both President
Eisenhower *and* his Mom for without
her there would have been no D-Day.

Nazi Germany never recovered.

mass destruction 1944

Hitler ended his rage
when he took his life.

Truman had become President,
and now he faced a big problem.
What to do with Japan?

We were thinking of invading,
but it would mean many lives lost.
And we did not want that.

So, we loaded up a plane with an
atomic bomb called "Little Boy."
It was dropped on Hiroshima.

Everything was destroyed.

Three days later, "Fat Man"
was dropped over Nagasaki.
Again, everything was destroyed.

Japan finally surrendered,
and signed the treaty that
ended World War II.

A nuclear bomb has never
again been used in a war.

Hiroshima:
August 6, 1945,
140,000 died

Nagasaki:
August 9, 1945,
80,000 died.

Japan surrendered
August 15, 1945

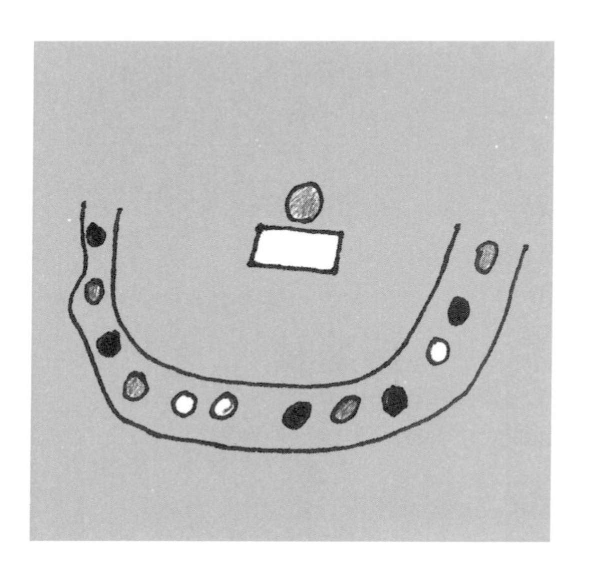

the world unites

1945

After we used the atomic bombs,
a really good thing happened. We
turned around to Japan and said,

"Here's our hand."

We also helped Germany. We knew
that we had to help them end their
economic problems after the war.

While all this was happening,
the United Nations was born.

Every country in the world comes
together to discuss things like
politics, peace, poverty, and hunger.

It is a good idea to be able to get
together and talk things over
before a war breaks out.

But, that does not always happen.

192 member
countries meet
throughout the
year at U.N.
Headquarters in
New York City.

Two of its most
effective agencies
are: UNICEF, the
children's fund;
and WHO, the World
Health Organization.

a curtain descends

1945-1960

Now, a new kind of war began.
We had to stop Communism
from taking over the world.

It began at Yalta. This was when
the Soviet Union got all of
Eastern Europe.

Winston Churchill called it the
"Iron Curtain." And it was a
very scary time for everyone!

Fear of nuclear weapons.
Bomb shelters.
Air raid drills.

Only five years after World War II
ended, America was at war again,
battling communists in Korea.

Dwight D. Eisenhower promised to
end the war if he became president.
And he did just that in 1953.

By then, 34,000 Americans, 900,000
Chinese and 2,000,000 Koreans had
lost their lives. What a waste!

Yalta Treaty
1945

Berlin Blockade
1948-49

NATO is created
1949

Communist China
1949

Korean War
1950-53

Hydrogen Bomb
1952

Soviets launch Sputnik
1957

U2 Affair
1956

Castro rules Cuba
1959

a true heroine

1955

She was born in 1913 in Tuskegee, Alabama. As a child, she did not understand why people of her color

were mistreated.

Rosa was a nurse and an activist. She said, "Jim Crow Laws are wrong, and we need to do something!"

This was in 1955. December First. Many took buses to work, and only whites were allowed to sit up front.

After work Rosa Parks and three other blacks sat down in the fifth row of a bus.

The driver told them to move to the back. Three moved, but Rosa stood her ground.

What a woman!

She told the bus driver that he could not tell her what to do. She said, "I am not moving!"

"People always say that I didn't give up my seat because I was tired, but that isn't true. I was not tired physically, or more tired than I usually was at the end of a working day. I was not old, although some people have an image of me as being old then. I was forty-two. No, the only tired I was, was tired of giving in."

- Rosa Parks
My Story

The bus driver called the police.
As they arrested Rosa she told them
that they were making a big mistake.

Her saying, “No!” inspired everybody
including Dr. Martin Luther King, Jr.

They held the Montgomery Bus
Boycott. And this was the beginning
of the Civil Rights movement.

When Rosa Parks died she was still
full of spunk. Her body was carried
to our nation’s Capitol to be honored.

Rosa Parks is one of my favorite
people in all of American history.
What she did inspired all of us.

EVEN MY HEART.

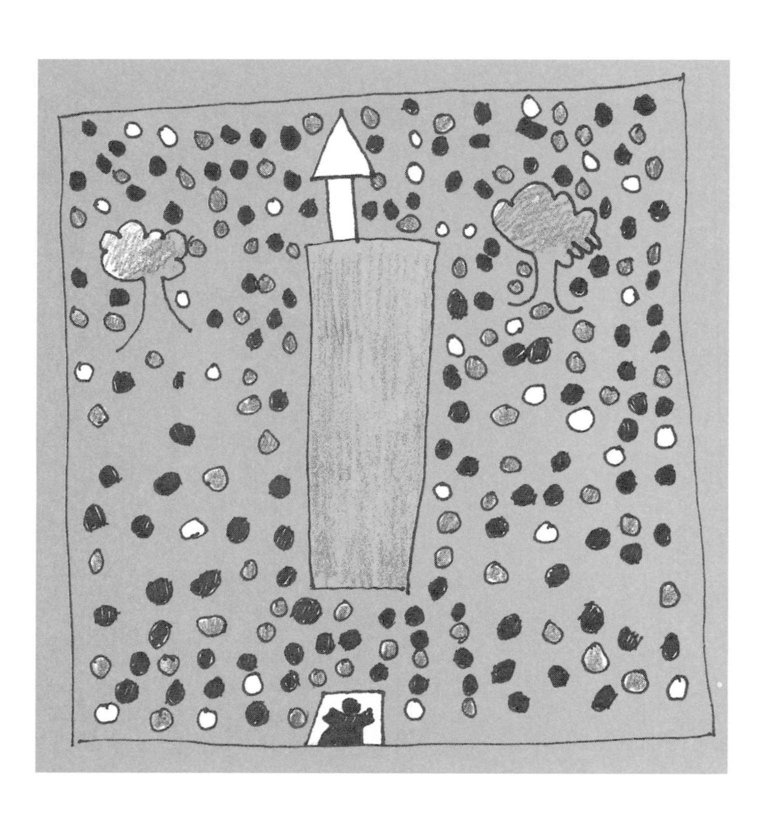

free at last!

1955-1968

When Rosa Parks was arrested, angry black leaders met. They were planning a boycott, and now they had a heroine.

They chose as their leader a young, unknown minister by the name of Dr. Martin Luther King, Jr.

Black churches were burned, and someone bombed Martin Luther King's home!

He asked us to stop all the fighting. "There are not whites and blacks," he said, "we are one."

This led to the biggest march ever in Washington, D.C. where King made his famous speech, "I have a dream."

And I know the ending:
"Free at last! Free at last! Thank God Almighty, we are free at last!"

When Dr. King was assassinated, riots broke out. We should have honored his memory better.

The Montgomery Bus Boycott lasted 371 days to December 20, 1956.

250,000 took part in the March on Washington, August 28, 1963.

President Johnson's Civil Rights Act of 1964 outlawed segregation in schools and public places.

Martin Luther King, Jr. was assassinated April 4, 1968.

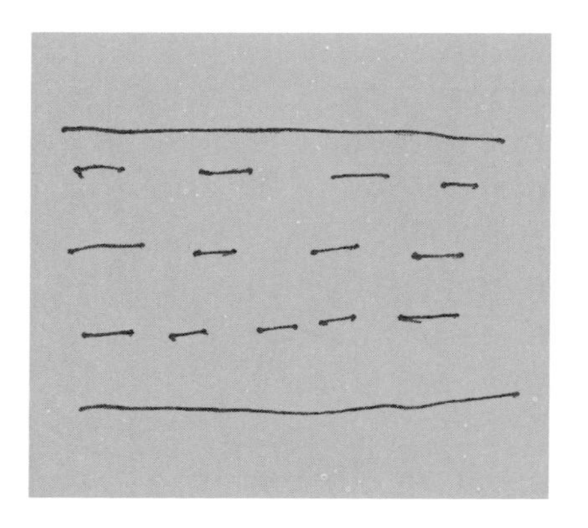

the cold war continues 1960-1980

The big fear was this:
if communists took over a
country, others would follow.

We did not want that to happen.

So, when communists in North
Vietnam invaded South Vietnam,
we went to war to stop them.

But, we did not know their
history, and we were not used
to fighting in jungles.

It was tragic.

We did not know how to get out.
There were huge protests all over
America, and we finally left in 1973.

When North Vietnam defeated
South Vietnam, they renamed
Saigon, Ho Chi Minh City.

"Each time the question of the domino theory was sent to intelligence experts for evaluation, they would send back answers which reflected their doubts about its validity, but the highest level of government left the domino theory alone. It was, as if, by questioning it, they might have revealed its emptiness, and would then have been forced to act on their new discovery."

- David Halberstam
  The Best and the Brightest

U-2 Incident
1960

U.S. invades
Bay of Pigs in Cuba
1961

Berlin Wall Built
1961

Cuban Missile Crisis
1962

Gulf of Tonkin incident
1964

U.S. troops to Vietnam
1965

U.S. fights Communists
in Dominican Republic
1965

Middle East Six Day War
1967

Soviets stop revolt
in Czechoslovakia
1968

Nixon to China
1972

Salt I Treaty signed
1972

U.S. leaves Vietnam
1973

Communists
take Cambodia
1975

North Vietnam
defeats South Vietnam
1975

Soviets invade
Afghanistan
1979

Salt II Treaty signed
1979

Iranian Hostage Crisis
1979 - 1980

four dead in ohio

1970

During the Vietnam War, a crowd
of students, at Kent State University
in Ohio, were protesting the war.

"Step back! Step Back!"
the National Guard ordered.

"No!" the students yelled back.

Suddenly, shots rang out,
and four young students
were dead.

During this time, there was
a band by the name of Crosby
Stills, Nash and Young.

Neil Young heard about this tragedy,
and thought that he should write
about the massacre and Vietnam.

The song is called "Ohio."

"Tin soldiers and
Nixon coming,
We're finally on
our own.
This summer I
hear the drumming,
Four dead in Ohio."

- Neil Young

national nightmare

1972

One night, a building in Washington called Watergate was robbed. It was Democratic Party headquarters.

Five men were arrested, and people wondered," What were they doing? It took two long years to find out.

During this long nightmare, President Richard Nixon, kept saying he had nothing to do with it.

"I am not a crook," he told the nation.

Well, he was lying. He actually was the one who ordered the break-in! A guy named Deep Throat knew this.

But, it was not until they found the tapes that they had proof. The truth came out and Nixon resigned.

What he put our nation through was unspeakable. He committed a crime, and took no responsibility for it.

"My fellow Americans, our long national nightmare is over."

- President Ford
  August 9, 1974

"That the way I tried to deal with Watergate was the wrong way is a burden I shall bear for every day of the life that is left to me."

- President Nixon,
  September 8, 1974

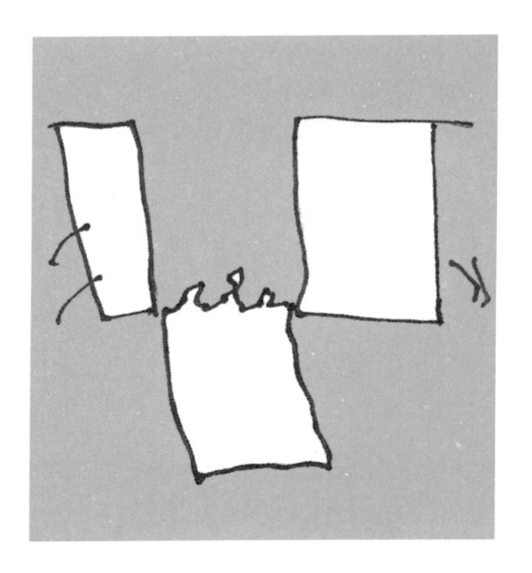

the wall falls!

1991

At this point in time, Ronald
Reagan was our president

He knew from experiences, such as
the Cuban Missile Crisis, that we had
to stop the use of nuclear weapons.

So, Reagan set up treaties with the
Soviet Union. But, he never once let up
his guard. He stood tall and strong.

When we heard the news about the
Berlin Wall falling, we all felt
a big sigh of relief.

The Soviet Empire ended thanks
to Ronald Reagan. I like how Colin
Powell put it. He said that his...

“total belief in the ultimate triumph
of democracy and freedom and his
willingness to act on that belief

helped end the Cold War and
usher in a new and brighter
phase of history.”

Solidarity in Poland
1980

President Reagan’s
Star Wars defense
1983

Gorbachev & Reagan
meet in Iceland
1986

US/USSR nuclear
arms agreement
1987

Berlin Wall falls
1989

Germany unifies
1990

Gorbachev ousted and
Soviet Union collapses
1991

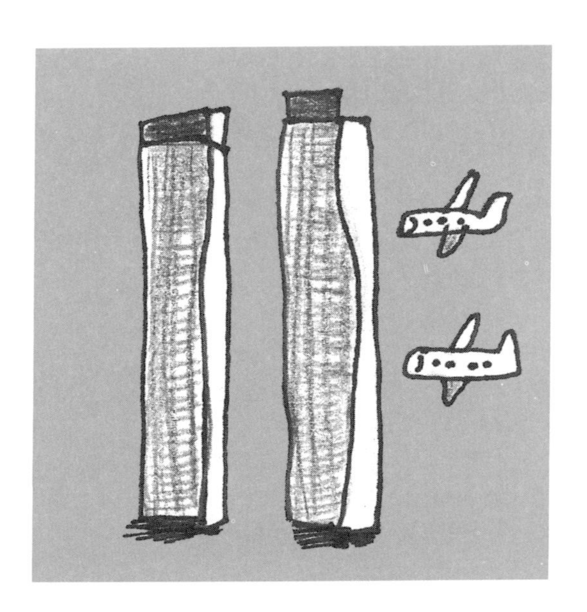

9/11 2001

Osama bin Laden was behind 9/11.
He was from Saudi Arabia.

He got his pilots into planes, and he told them to fly into New York's two biggest buildings.

The Twin Towers crashed to the ground.

Many people lost their lives. And as I look back on it now, I am going to choke up. My cousin is a firefighter,

and he was there.

This was the beginning of the War on Terror.

"Time is passing. Yet, for the United States of America there will be no forgetting September the 11th. We will remember every rescuer who died in honor.We will remember every family that lives in grief."

- President George W. Bush, Novmber 11, 2001

iraq

2002

If we start a war like Iraq,
we need to realize what
we are doing.

We do not know Iraq's history.

Iraq had nothing to do with 9/11.
The terrorists were from
Saudi Arabia.

The U.N. did not want
war in Iraq, but we
did it anyway.

Our soldiers are sacrificing their
lives to make the world better.
I think they are beginning to say,

"Bring us home. Now.
We have a reason to live,

not to die."

"The immediate reason that Mr. Bush opened Pandora's box in the Middle East and invaded Iraq was his moral certitude that Saddam Hussein had weapons of mass destruction and that he was working in close partnership with Osama bin Laden and al-Qa'ida. Those convictions turned out to be delusions."

- Arthur Schlesinger
The Independent/UK
April 15, 2004

my biggest
concerns

war

This is an on-going thing, from
the Revolutionary War to Iraq.
They all start over arguments.

We should get together and say,
"Yes, we have disagreements,
but can we work it out?"

Instead, we keep making the
same mistakes because we
do not remember the past.

We go to war when
we do not have to.

History teaches that
the stress within us gets
released into killing.

Our country needs one good
massage. This will relieve the
stress, and there will be peace.

Actually, the whole world
needs one huge massage.

our health

Health in our country is in
bad shape. Too many people
do not have health coverage.

And there is too much obesity.
Being overweight leads to
obesity, that leads to death.

The diseases and side effects are
severe. Diabetes, heart disease,
and high blood pressure.

We should stop eating bad
things, and start eating more
fruits and vegetables.

And we should exercise.

Too many Americans have
excuses to not exercise.
And do you know what?

We are using ourselves

as bait.

global warming

One of the movies that I saw was
An *Inconvenient Truth* by Al Gore.
What the movie said was this:

We cannot let earth's animals die.
We cannot let our forests die.
We need to recycle. Reuse.

We need to save electricity.
Too many leave the lights on.
They just don't get it.

We all must take part in saving
our environment. Take a stand.
Go to Congress and say,

"Stop the pollution!"

If we do that, and we act
now, we will be able to
save our

God's creation.

Earth teach me courage -
as the tree that stands alone.

Earth teach me limitation -
as the ant that crawls on the ground.

Earth teach me freedom -
as the eagle that soars in the sky.

Earth teach me acceptance -
as the leaves that die each fall.

Earth teach me renewal -
as the seed that rises in the spring.

- From an Ute prayer

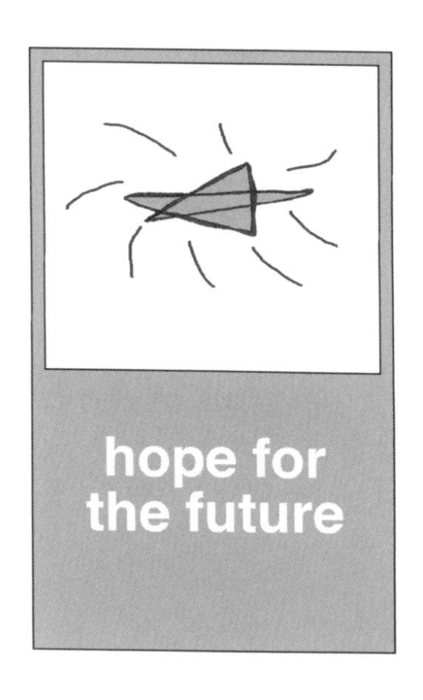
hope for
the future

WE HIDE
BEHIND OUR
FREEDOM

Freedom to some people
is only a word. But, to me,
it is more than that.

We, the citizens of the
U.S.A., have freedom
in everything we do.

But, war is not one of them.

We are scared of the fact that
we are going out and making
the same mistakes as before.

That is why we hide.

When we hide we are
not aware of what is going
on in the real world.

Diseases. Global warming.
Our economy is a mess. Our
foreign policy is crumbling.

Look at where we are.

responsibility

Respect the law.

Freedom does not mean
mean that you are free
to hurt other people.

listening

If we start an argument,
we must finish it.
Right away.

We need to listen to one
another. Stop and ask,

"What were you going to say?"

a higher power

We Americans are very religious. We worship God in different ways. And that is O.K.

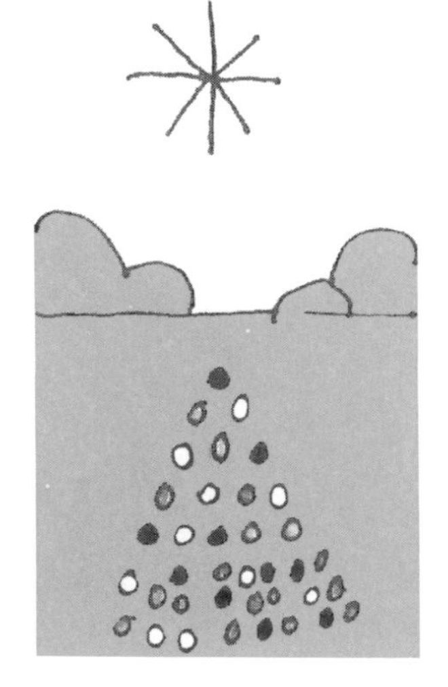

As the Great Awakenings taught us, we can practice our religions freely.

It does not matter if we are Christians or Jews, Muslims or Buddhists.

When we pray, we do it with respect. We dig deep within ourselves, and say,

"I believe."

Connor at age 5

hope

America is the land of hope.
The land of freedom,
and the future.

What happened in the past,
we cannot undo. What we can
do is prevent future problems.

What we went through—
our past and our tribulations—
are crossing the skies.

We can change the world.
Find cures for diseases.
Make our earth clean.

America is going to come back.
Oh, Yes!

God Bless the

U. S. of A!

Be the change

you want to see

in the world.

- Mahatma Gandhi

AMERICA
according to
CONNOR GIFFORD

Reader Group

Questions and

Topics for Discussion

CONNOR'S WORDS

What does Tim Russert mean when he says that Connor has "a unique perspective" of American history?

What are the major themes that Connor discusses throughout the book?

Why does Connor believe that it is so critical that we know our country's history?

Do we need to change the way history is taught in schools today?

What were your favorite profiles.

What did you learn that most surprised you? Moved you?

IN THE BEGINNING

What major themes are introduced in the first section that then appear throughout American history?

In Connor's view, who was our Founding Mother? Who else qualifies for this honor?

Connor believes that Ben Franklin is our most underrated leader? Does anyone else fit this description?

How did women impact the founding of America?

What role did religion play?

What role did arguments play?

GROWING PAINS

What led to westward expansion
and what impact did it have on
the first half of the 19th century?

Discuss key people and events
in the struggle for equal rights.

What does Connor think
"Separate but Equal" means?

How did religion impact the
lives of Americans in the 1800's?
What role does it play today?

Is Connor especially sensitive
to those who are "different?"

AMERICA TAKES THE LEAD

How did America's rapid growth impact social and economic issues at the turn of the century?

Discuss why America entered four wars in the 20th century, and whether they were justified.

Compare Shaw's Regiment in the Civil War with the Tuskagee airmen in World War II.

What are the similarities between George Washington and Dwight D. Eisenhower?

What were key events that ended Separate but Equal as the Law of the Land?

What upsets Connor about Nixon? Do you see similarities in any politicians today?

Was the use of the atomic bomb to end the war in Japan justifed?

What led to the Cold War and how did it end?

Do you agree with Connor's view of the war in Iraq?

MY BIGGEST CONCERNS

How do your biggest concerns compare with Connor's?

HOPE FOR THE FUTURE

Discuss "We hide behind our our freedom" and Connor's other views in this section.

CONNOR'S ART

What are your favorite drawings?
How do they complement his words?

What do the circles in his drawings represent, and how do they change? Compare the drawings on page 60 with 82; and page 70 with 137.

How do the drawings on pages 13, 47 and 79 differ from one another?

Why is the ink spilled in the drawing of the Declaration of Independence?

Discover
the wonders of
CONNOR'S WORLD
at connorgifford.com

Join his blog, read his newsletter,
follow his American journey.